FACT CAT

FRUIT AND VEGETABLES

Izzi Howell

FACT CAT

Get your paws on this fantastic new mega-series from Wayland!

Join our Fact Cat on a journey of fun learning about every subject under the sun!

First published in paperback in Great Britain in 2020 by Wayland
Copyright © Hodder and Stoughton Limited, 2017

ISBN: 978 1 5263 0354 7

10 9 8 7 6 5 4 3 2 1

MIX
Paper from responsible sources
FSC® C104740
www.fsc.org

Wayland
An imprint of Hachette Children's Group
Part of Hodder & Stoughton
Carmelite House
50 Victoria Embankment
London EC4Y 0DZ

An Hachette UK Company
www.hachette.co.uk
www.hachettechildrens.co.uk

A catalogue for this title is available from the British Library
Printed and bound in Dubai

Produced for Wayland by White-Thomson Publishing Ltd
www.wtpub.co.uk

Editor: Izzi Howell
Design: Clare Nicholas
Fact Cat illustrations: Shutterstock/Julien Troneur
Other illustrations: Stefan Chabluk
Consultant: Karina Philip

Picture and illustration credits:
iStock: Anna_Shepulova 5, fstop123 6, pkstock 8b, subman 10, Nicole S. Young 17, Okea 18tl, eli_asenova 18tr, Anna Kucherova 18br, alpaksoy 20l, JoepvdW 21tl; Shutterstock: sisqopote cover, images72 title page and 12, Romariolen 4, Helen Sushitskaya 7, sta 8t, Steve Allen 9, Kazyavka 9, bergamont 9, Daxiao Productions 9, blueeyes 9, imaged 9, Kingarion 11, Tiplyashina Evgeniya 13, Brent Hofacker 14, Foodio 15, Billion Photos 16, NIPAPORN PANYACHAROEN 18b, focuslight 18bl, Wanwisspaul 19, Daniel Novoa 20r, nito 21tr, puwanai 21b.
Should there be any inadvertent omission, please apply to the publisher for rectification.

The author, Izzi Howell, is a writer and editor specialising in children's educational publishing.

The consultant, Karina Philip, is a teacher and a primary literacy consultant with an MA in creative writing.

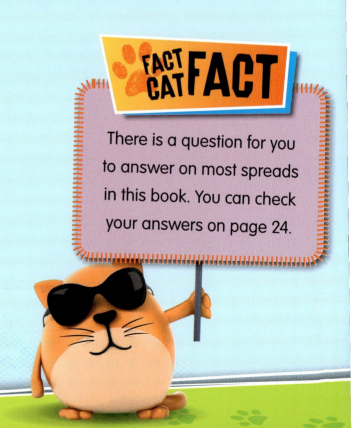

FACT CAT FACT

There is a question for you to answer on most spreads in this book. You can check your answers on page 24.

CONTENTS

What are fruit and vegetables?..4

Different vegetables..............6

Types of fruit...................8

Farming 10

Growing fruit..................12

Cooking.......................14

Fibre and vitamins.............16

A balanced diet 18

Around the world 20

Quiz..........................22

Glossary......................23

Index.........................24

Answers.......................24

WHAT ARE FRUIT AND VEGETABLES?

Fruit and vegetables are types of food. They come from plants.

Greengrocers sell fruit and vegetables. Fruit and vegetables come in many different shapes and sizes.

Fruit grows from flowers. It has seeds or a stone inside. It is usually sweet. Vegetables come from any other part of a plant. We mostly eat vegetables in **savoury** meals.

This savoury pasta dish is made with broccoli, courgette and tomato.

FACT CAT FACT

Tomatoes are actually fruit, because they have seeds inside them. However, most people use the word vegetable to describe tomatoes. Can you think of another vegetable with seeds that is actually a fruit?

DIFFERENT VEGETABLES

Some vegetables, such as carrots and potatoes, grow underground. They are part of the roots of the plant.

When radishes are picked, they are covered in soil from the ground. We need to wash them before we eat them.

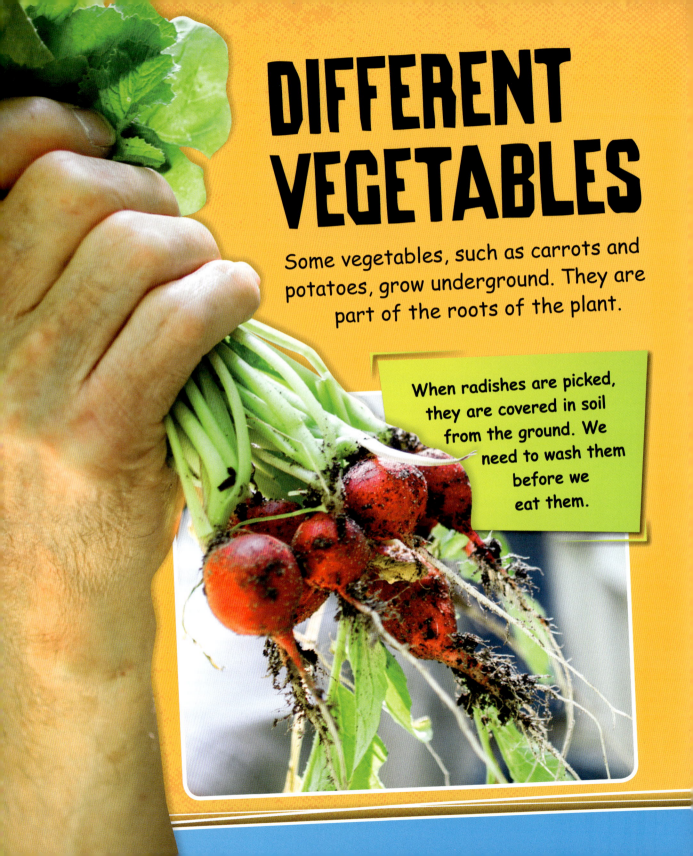

Some vegetables are the leaves and stems of plants. These vegetables are usually green. They include spinach and lettuce.

We eat the leaves of the cabbage plant. As well as green, what other colour can a cabbage be?

FACT CAT FACT

In the past, carrots weren't orange! They were purple or yellow. The first orange carrots were grown around 300 years ago.

TYPES OF FRUIT

Fruit comes in many sizes and shapes. Some berries, such as blueberries, are small. The watermelon is a large and heavy fruit.

Bananas are long, thin fruit. Most other types of fruit are round.

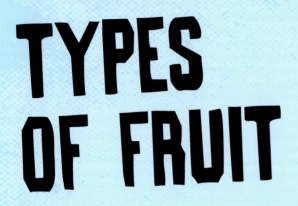

seed

There are many colours of fruit. Sometimes, the skin of a fruit is a different colour from the inside. For example, kiwis have brown skin, but they are bright green inside.

Fruit comes in every colour of the rainbow. Can you think of two more red fruits?

cherries

grapes

blueberries

apples

mango

oranges

FARMING

Farmers plant vegetable seeds in fields. They water the seeds and **weed** the field so that the plants have space to grow. After a few months, the vegetables are ready to **harvest**.

This farmer is harvesting lettuce from the field. Usually, only one type of vegetable is planted in each field.

FACT CAT FACT

Some farmers use **pesticides** to stop insects from eating their **crops**. This is bad for the **environment**. Which word describes vegetables and fruit that are grown without chemicals?

Some plants, such as peppers, only grow in warm weather. Farmers grow these plants in greenhouses, which are warm inside. This means that they can pick vegetables all year round.

Tomatoes need warm weather to grow. They are often planted in greenhouses.

GROWING FRUIT

Some fruits, such as lemons and plums, grow on trees. Raspberries and blackberries grow on small plants that are close to the ground.

Farmers plant apple trees together in an orchard. In which season are apples ready to be picked?

Most fruit is picked when it is nearly **ripe**. It takes a long time for the fruit to travel from the farm to the supermarket. By the time the fruit reaches the supermarket, it is ripe and ready to eat.

Strawberries are soft and **delicate**. They are picked by hand so that they don't get damaged.

FACT CAT FACT

Tropical fruits, such as pineapples, mangoes and bananas, only grow in hot countries. These fruits are sent around the world on planes and boats. This means that people in colder countries can eat them too.

COOKING

Most fruit can be eaten **raw**. Cooking fruit makes it softer. Apples are crunchy when they are raw, but soft when they are cooked.

We sometimes use cooked fruit in desserts, such as cherry pie.

FACT CAT FACT

If you squeeze or press fruit or vegetables, juice comes out. We often drink juice from oranges and apples. You can also make juice from tomatoes and cucumbers!

Many types of vegetables, such as carrots, can be eaten raw or cooked. Cooking vegetables changes their taste and **texture**. Some vegetables, such as potatoes, have to be cooked before they can be eaten.

Always check with an adult before eating raw fruit or vegetables.

We often eat raw vegetables in salads.

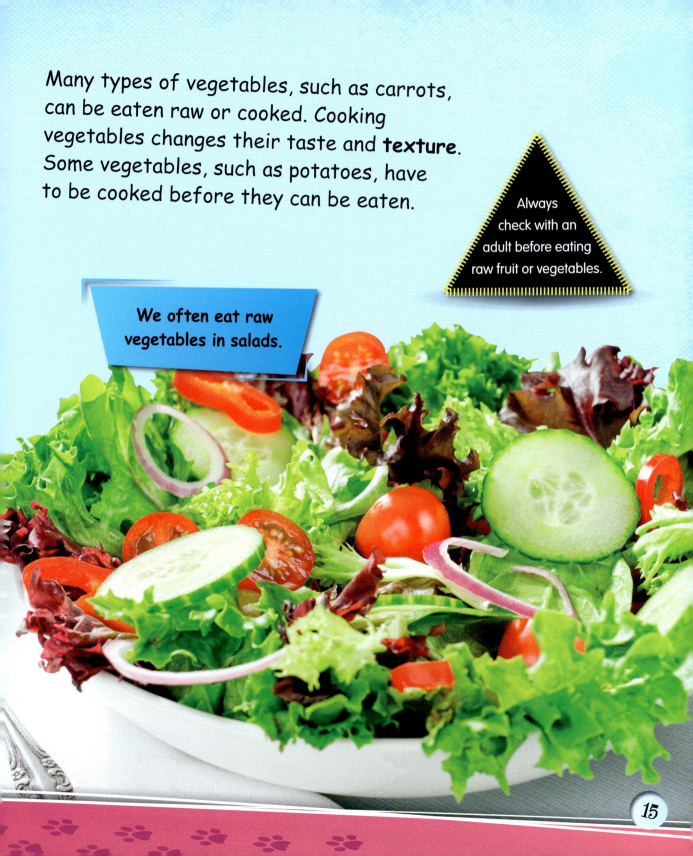

FIBRE AND VITAMINS

Some fruits, such as apples and bananas, contain **fibre**. Fibre is good for your **digestion**. There is also fibre in vegetables, such as carrots.

Fibre is only found in food that comes from plants, such as figs.

Fruit and vegetables contain different **vitamins** and **minerals**. Vitamins and minerals help to keep your body healthy.

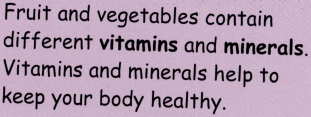

Dark-green leafy vegetables, such as broccoli, contain Vitamin K and the mineral, iron. Vitamin K helps cuts to heal properly. Iron is good for your blood.

FACT CAT FACT

Not all vitamins come from fruit and vegetables. Most of the Vitamin D that we need comes from sunlight! Vitamin D makes our bones and teeth healthy. How many vitamins are there?

A BALANCED DIET

A **balanced diet** is made up of different types of food. You also need to eat the right amount of food from each food group. Vegetables and fruit are an example of a food group.

seven small tomatoes

a glass of orange juice

These are all **portions** of fruit and vegetables. You should eat at least five portions of fruit and vegetables every day.

two spears of broccoli

three large spoonfuls of peas

a pear

This diagram shows you how much of each type of food you should eat. The large parts of the circle show foods you should eat at most meals. The small parts of the circle show foods you should eat less often.

Vegetables and fruit are in this part of the circle. You should eat fruit and vegetables at almost every meal.

Fruit and vegetables

Grains and cereals

Meat, fish and eggs

Oil and butter

Dairy products

AROUND THE WORLD

Every country has its own dishes made from **local** fruit and vegetables. In some places, people cook the same fruit and vegetables in different ways.

In Turkey, they fill aubergines with onions, tomatoes and **minced meat.**

In China, aubergines are cooked with spicy chilli and soy sauce.

Nopales are cactus leaves with the spines removed.

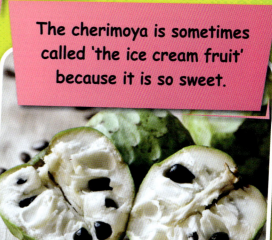

The cherimoya is sometimes called 'the ice cream fruit' because it is so sweet.

Some fruits and vegetables are hard to find in other countries. They have different **flavours** and textures, but they still contain vitamins and minerals.

Inside the hard skin of the durian, the fruit is creamy and tasty.

FACT CAT FACT

Durian is the smelliest fruit in the world! It smells like sweaty socks and rotten eggs. In some countries, you are not allowed to eat durian on buses or trains.

QUIZ

Try to answer the questions below. Look back through the book to help you. Check your answers on page 24.

1 Carrots grow above the ground? True or not true?

a) true

b) not true

2 Which fruit has brown skin and is green inside?

a) kiwi

b) mango

c) grapefruit

3 Cooking fruit makes it crunchy. True or not true?

a) true

b) not true

4 Vitamins are good for your body. True or not true?

a) true

b) not true

5 How many portions of fruit and vegetables should you eat every day?

a) one

b) ten

c) five

6 Nopales are cactus leaves. True or not true?

a) true

b) not true

GLOSSARY

balanced diet a diet that has a healthy mixture of different foods

crops a fruit or vegetable that a farmer grows in large amounts

delicate describes something that can break easily

digestion when your body uses the food in your stomach as energy

environment the air, land and water where people, animals and plants live

flavour the taste of a food or drink

fibre something found in food that your body needs for digestion

greengrocer a person who has a shop that sells fruit and vegetables

harvest to collect crops that are ready to eat

local describes something that comes from the area near you

minced meat meat cut into very tiny pieces

mineral something found in food that your body needs to be healthy

orchard a group of fruit trees in the same place

pesticide something that is used to kill insects that eat crops

portion an amount of food that is eaten at one time

raw not cooked

ripe describes a fruit or vegetable that is ready to be eaten

savoury a savoury dish is not sweet

texture the way that something feels

vitamin something found in food that your body needs to be healthy

weed to take away plants that you do not want growing in an area

INDEX

apples 9, 12, 14, 16

balanced diet 18–19
bananas 8, 13, 16
broccoli 5, 17

cabbage 7
carrots 6, 7, 15, 16

farmers 10, 11, 12
fibre 16
flowers 5

greengrocers 4
greenhouses 11

juice 14, 18

leaves 7, 17, 21
lettuce 7, 10, 11

orchards 12

potatoes 6, 15

raw fruit and
  vegetables 14–15
roots 6

seeds 5, 8, 10
stems 7

tomatoes 5, 11, 14, 18
trees 12
tropical fruit 13, 21

vitamins 17, 21

ANSWERS

Pages 4–17

Page 5: Some examples include cucumbers, courgettes and pumpkins.

Page 7: Red/purple

Page 9: Some fruits are apples, strawberries and plums.

Page 11: Organic

Page 12: Autumn

Page 17: Thirteen

Quiz answers

1   not true – they grow underground.

2   a – kiwi

3   not true – it makes the fruit soft.

4   true

5   c – five

6   true